Goodnight Paw...

This is the story of a unique little island on the South Carolina coast. It was first settled by rice planters that lived on plantations near the Waccamaw River. European settler Percival Pawley came to the Waccamaw Neck in the 1700s and started the development of our arrogantly shabby island. It is now one of the oldest summer resorts on the east coast. People come from far and near to enjoy this Island heaven. I grew up here and I know there is nothing like it.

— Flo Phillips

Written by
Flo Phillips

Flo Phillips

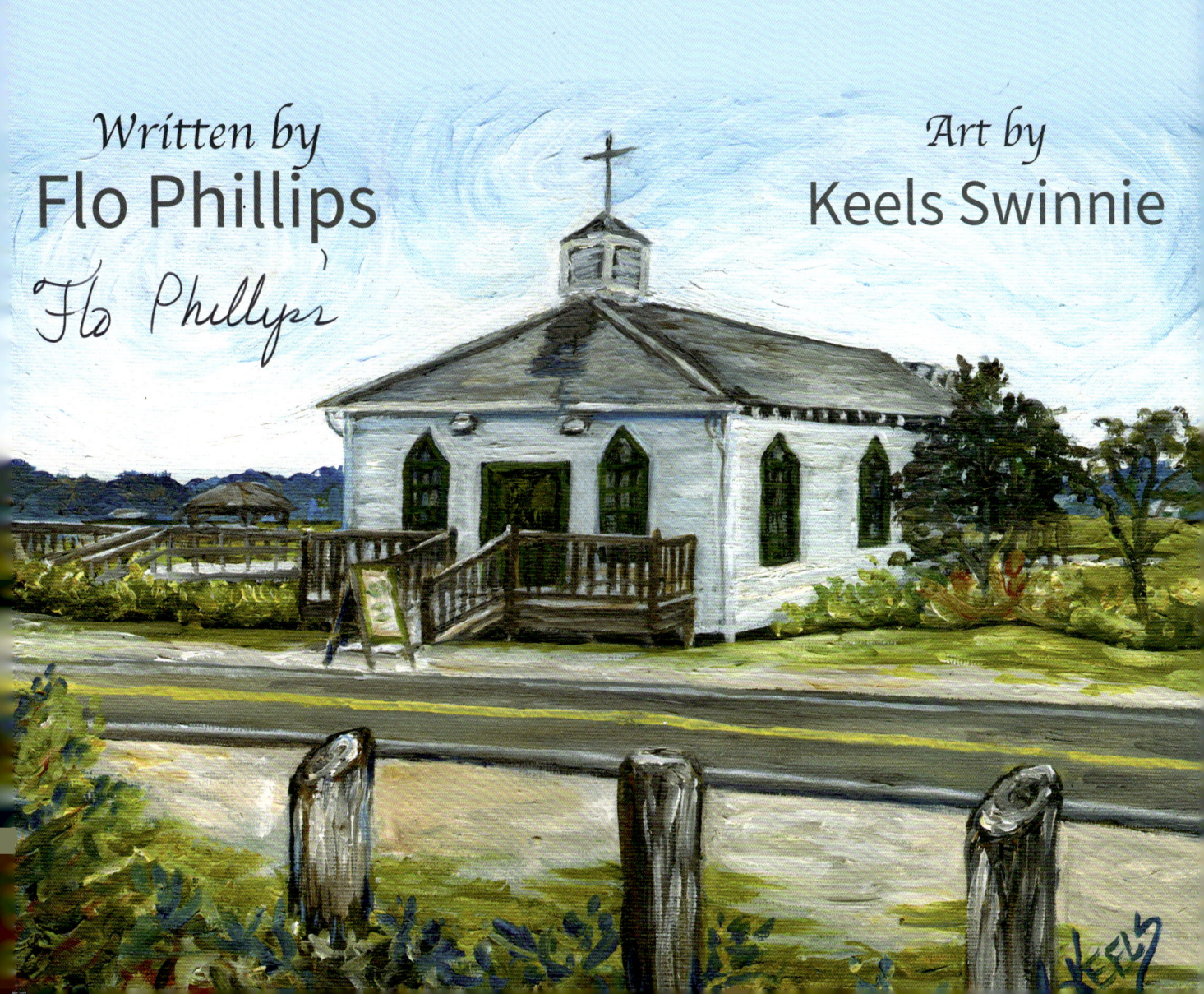

Art by
Keels Swinnie

Miss Flo

Floride Miller Phillips affectionately known as "Miss Flo" has been involved in the education, well being, and entertainment of children for decades. She currently enjoys tutoring, hosting manners classes, and summer enrichment camps in her home. Her husband, five dogs, two cats, and many hens and chicks add to the fun. Much of her life has been spent at **PAWLEYS** with her children and family. This book depicts many of their memories and those of other families that have loved this beautiful Island.

Her desire is that families enjoy this book together and create their own happy memories on this special little island.

Please involve your children in rhyming words, beautiful illustrations, and finding the hidden **PAWLEYS** Island shells.

Pawleys Island Shell

Pay attention, kids, we have a mystery.
The PAWLEYS shells are hiding where we can't see.
Listen to the story, but look and look.
Find them hidden in this little book.

What is a PAWLEYS Island Shell?

They are lovely little shells that beachcombers have been picking up for years at PAWLEYS. Their real name is the Imperial Venus Clam. Most locals don't know the proper name or just refuse to call them anything but PAWLEYS shells.

As soon as a prominent jeweler began making beautiful gold and silver jewelry out of them these little shells became the super stars of the strand. Everyone and their grandmamas search for them from morning until night. Once you learn to identify them you are hooked. There will be no more healthy jogs on the beach or hand-in-hand peaceful strolls. You will be on a mission and in a competition with others to find those intriguing little shells.

(For the grownups)
The Imperial Venus Clam is the true name of the PAWLEYS Island shell. They have unique ridges with deep furrows. Most of them are cream to grayish color with hints of brown. Although some claim that they are only found in Pawleys Island, these beautiful shells have been found from North Carolina to Texas and on the beaches in the West Indies.

As the sun sets on our beautiful PAWLEYS Island we begin to say our

Goodnights.

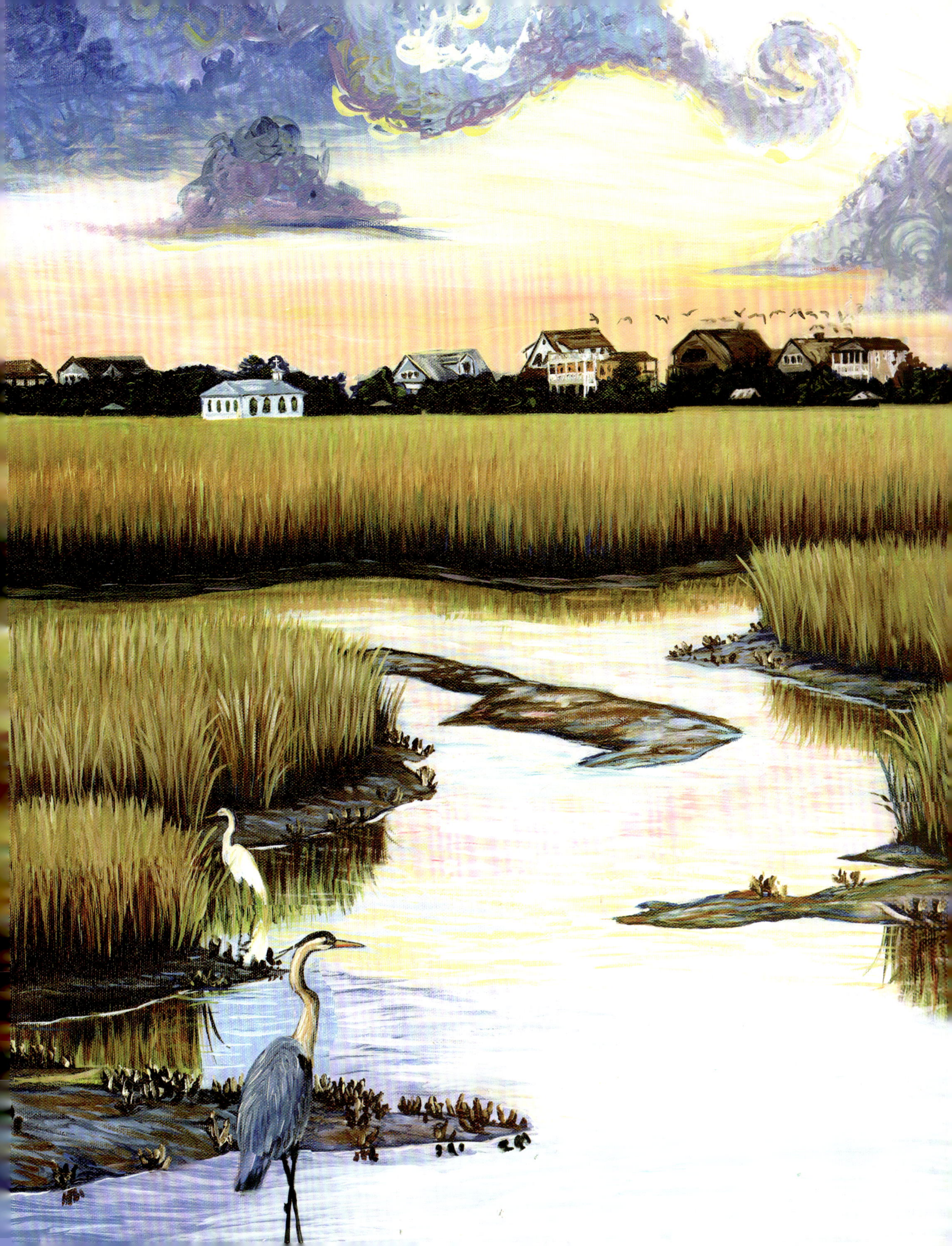

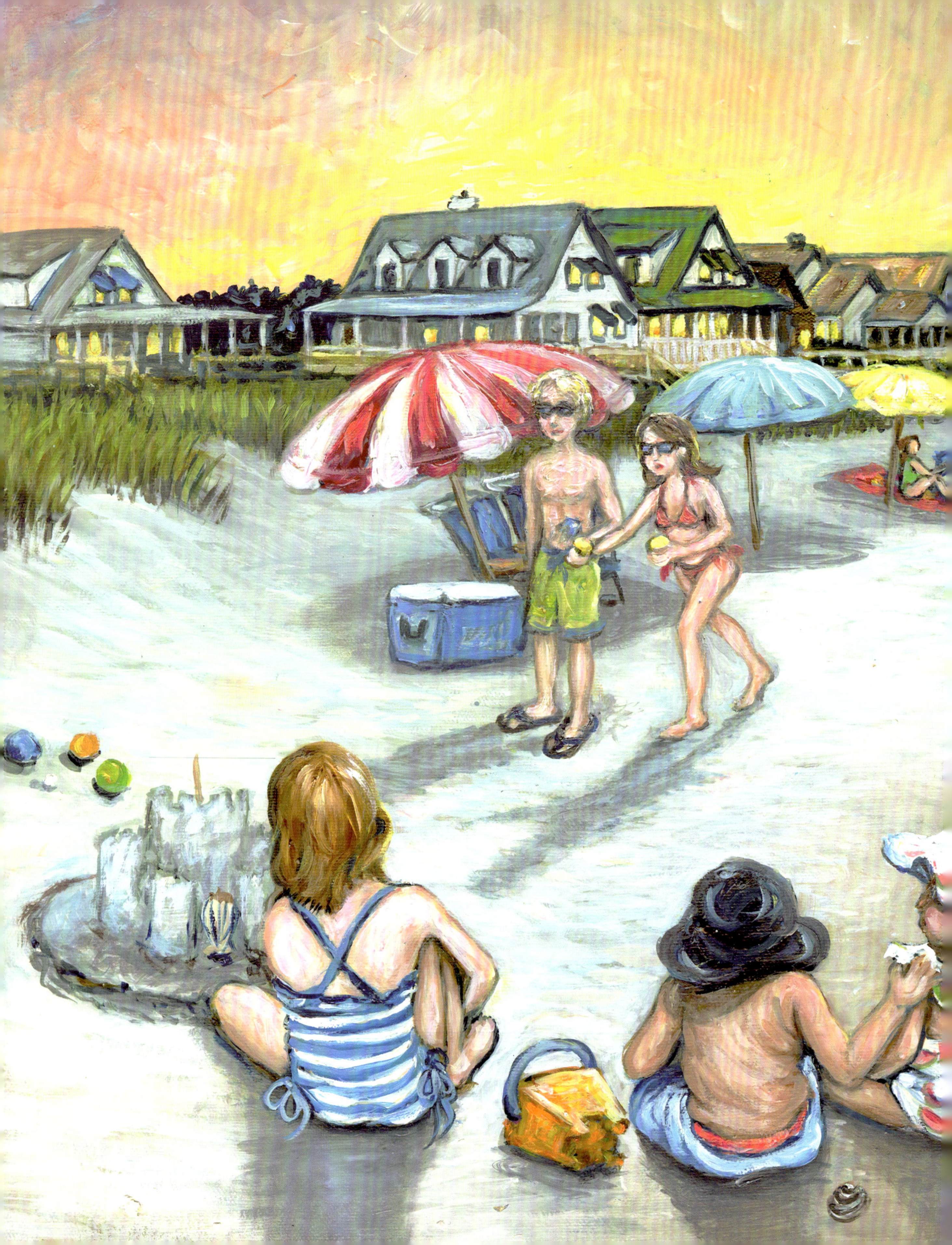

Goodnight swimming and surfing, lounging by the pier. You'll find some PAWLEYS Island shells, do not fear. Flying kites and frisbees too, bocci ball to name a few. Playing on the beach is so much fun as long as you don't get too much sun.

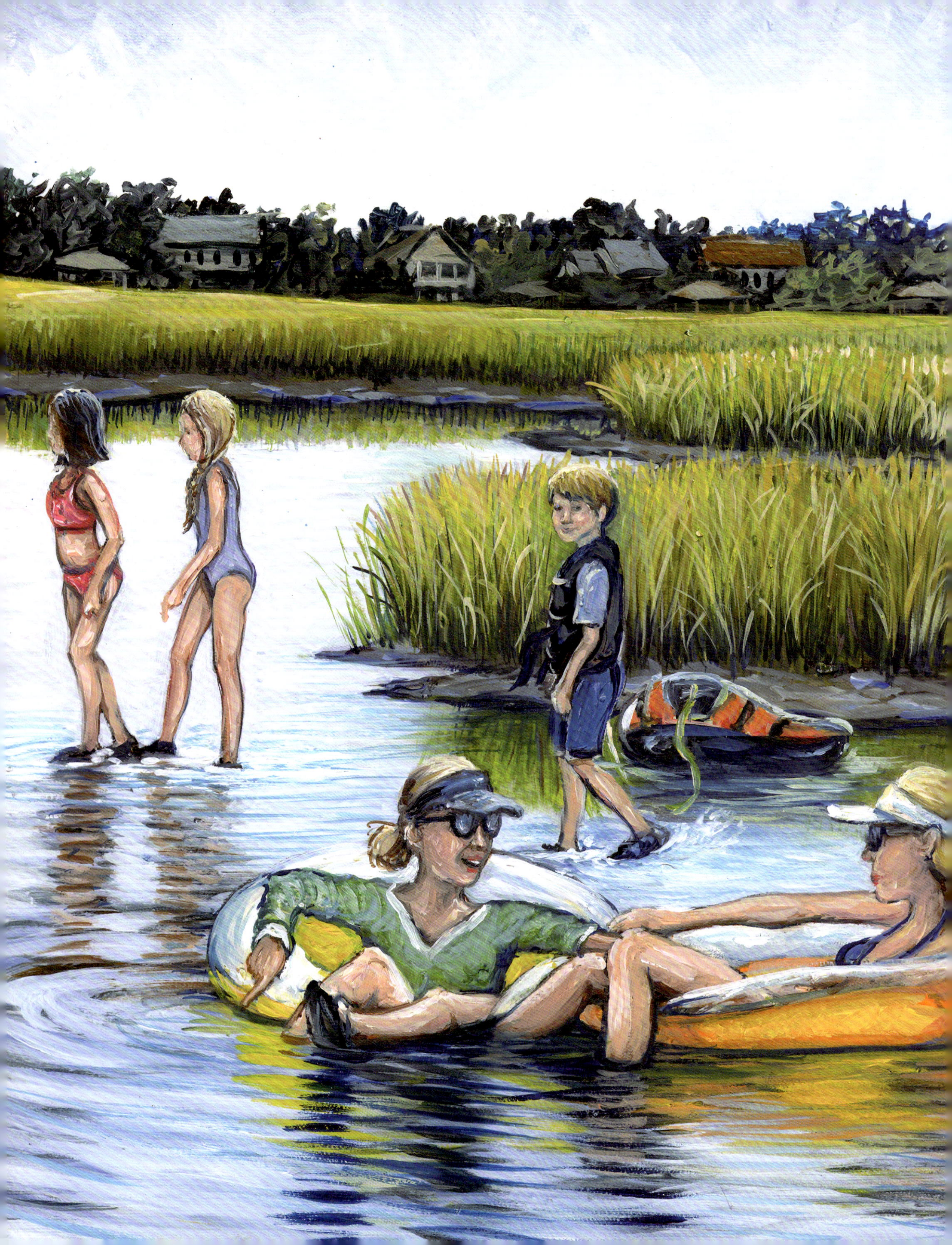

Goodnight little chapel and floating down the creek, what a peaceful way to enjoy your week. There's pluff mud, creek shoes, fishing and crabbing, just so many creatures out there for grabbing.

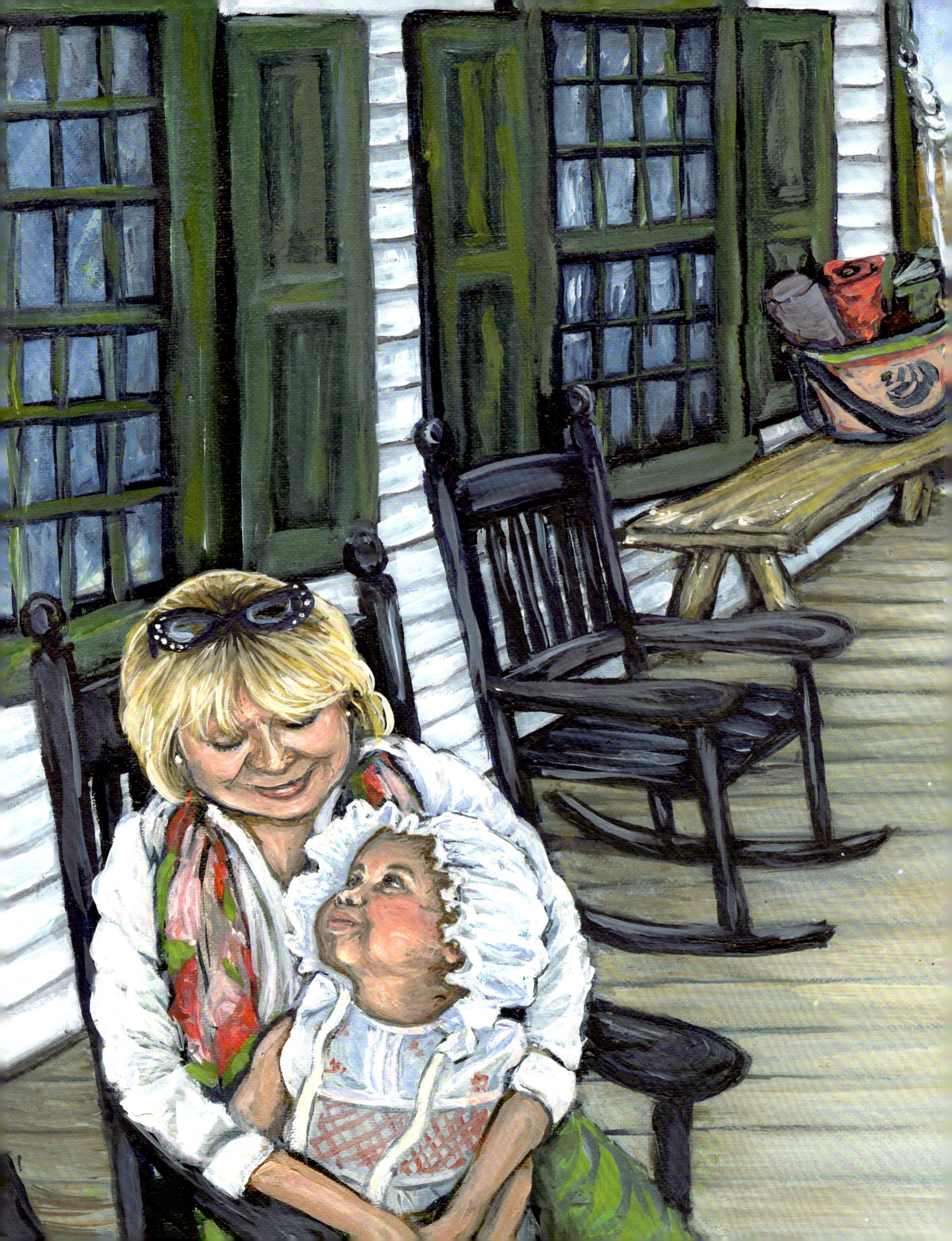

Goodnight screened porch, the perfect place to rest, snoozing in the hammock is really quite the best. Talking with friends and family with a grandchild on your lap, catching up with each other then take a little nap.

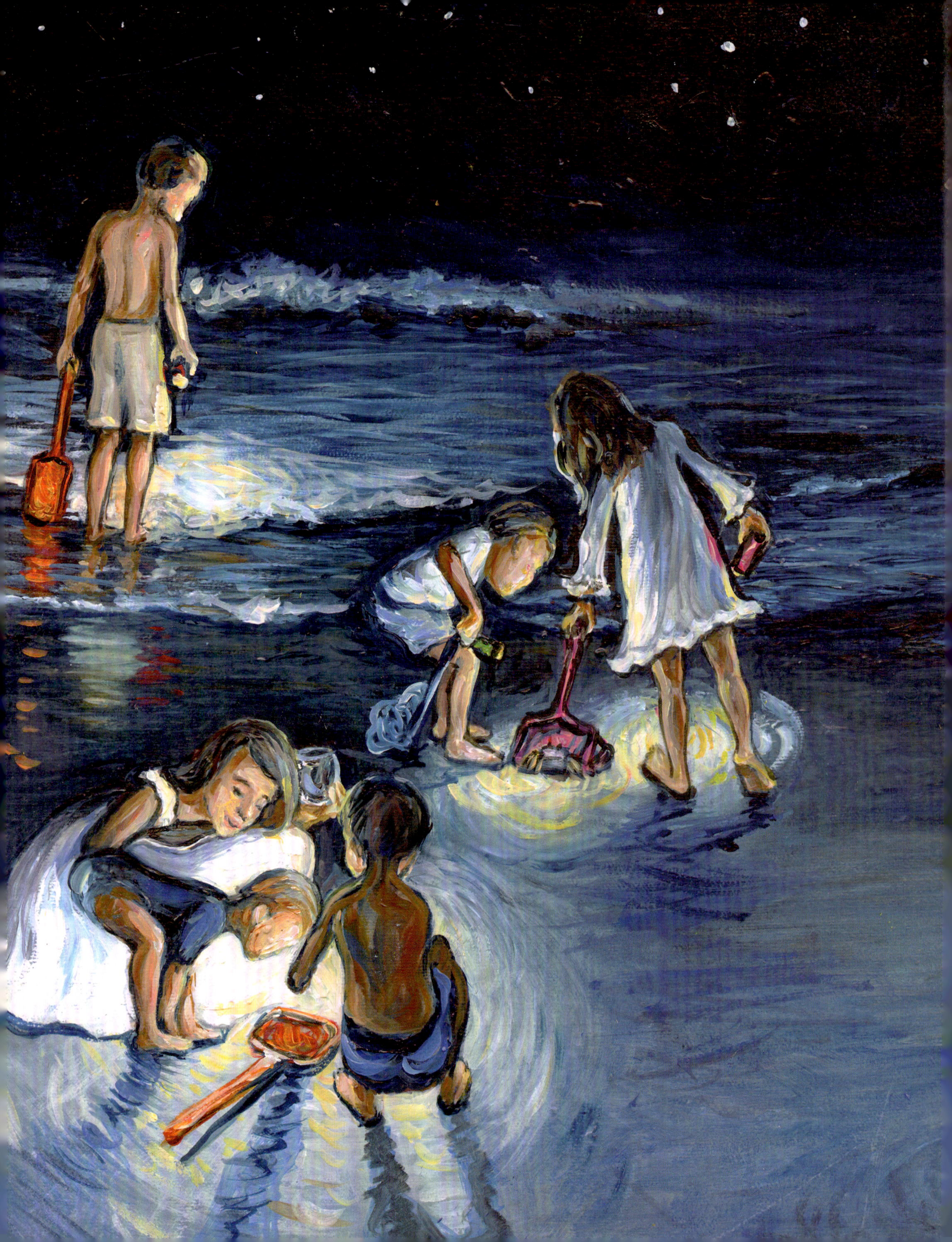

Goodnight sun kissed kids who always scream and shout, ghost crabs and turtles want to come out. Level out the sand and turn out the lights. Sweet Mama turtle might lay her eggs tonight.

Goodnight **Alice of the Hermitage and the Grayman ghost, the infamous spirits of our beloved coast. Don't be afraid, do not fear, these friendly ghosts are really quite dear. If you see a man in Gray strolling on the strand, he may be there to warn you and help protect your land.**

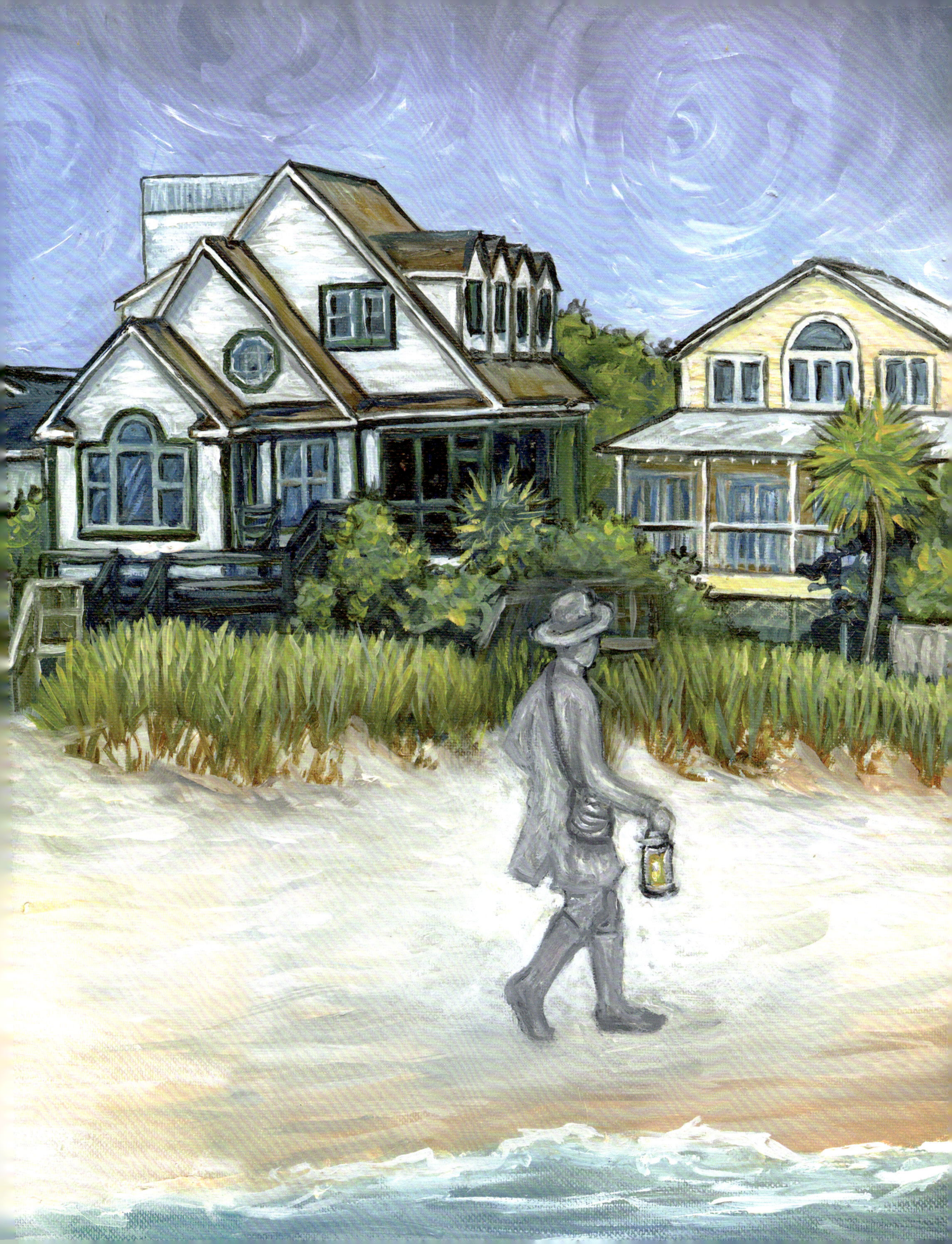

Goodnight

PAWLEYS inns,
proud as they can be,
overlooking the marsh and
gazing at the sea.

Through the years many
homes have changed,
but these quaint inns have
stayed the same.

Now only two inns are left on the strand. The surge from Hugo was too strong to withstand.

The Pelican and Seaview are thriving you see, but the Tip Top Inn is a sweet memory.

HUGO

Goodnight oyster roasts, shrimp boils and seafood so yummy, hush puppies and tomato pies filling our tummy.

There's juicy cold watermelon and ice cream treats,
but that delicious peach pie just can't be beat.

Goodnight cooking and washing dishes. Let our restaurants at **PAWLEYS** grant all your wishes. If you've had a fun beach day, don't want to cook, call for reservations and reserve a little nook. Great food and atmosphere, service with a smile. No other restaurants can compare. They go the extra mile!

217 BISTRO

PAWLEYS ISLAND
RUSTIC TABLE

Chive Blossom
Cafe
lunch dinner
237-1438

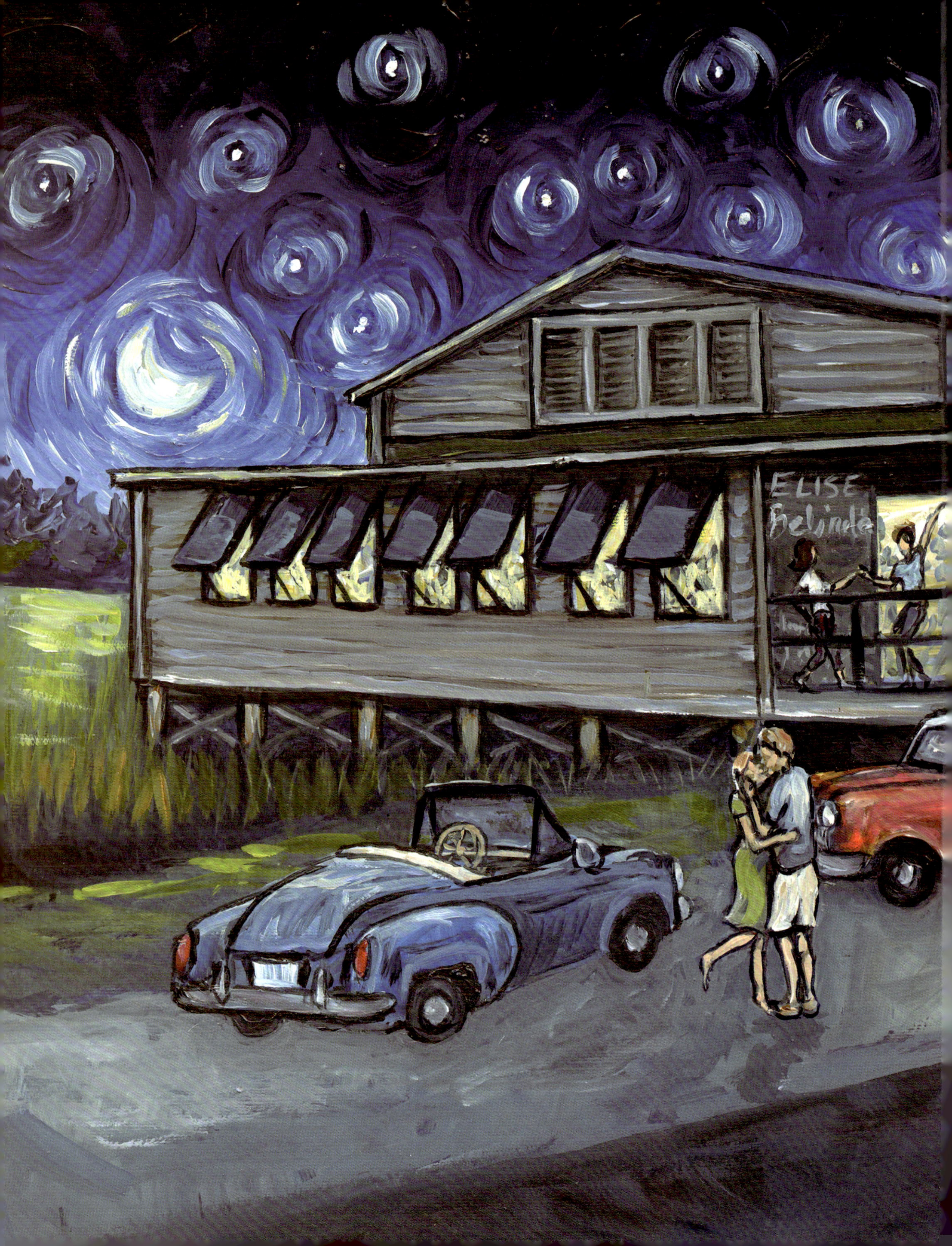
ELISE
Belinda

Goodnight **PAWLEYS** Pavilion or the place where it stood. Memories of bands and shaggers and those that thought they could. Guys meeting Gals and sneaking on the strand, stealing little kisses, and walking hand in hand.

Goodnight PAWLEYS marsh and creeking all the day. Making time for kids, when all of you can play. Leaving your worries back at home, spending time together. Swimming, splashing, laughing and giggling, these memories will last forever.

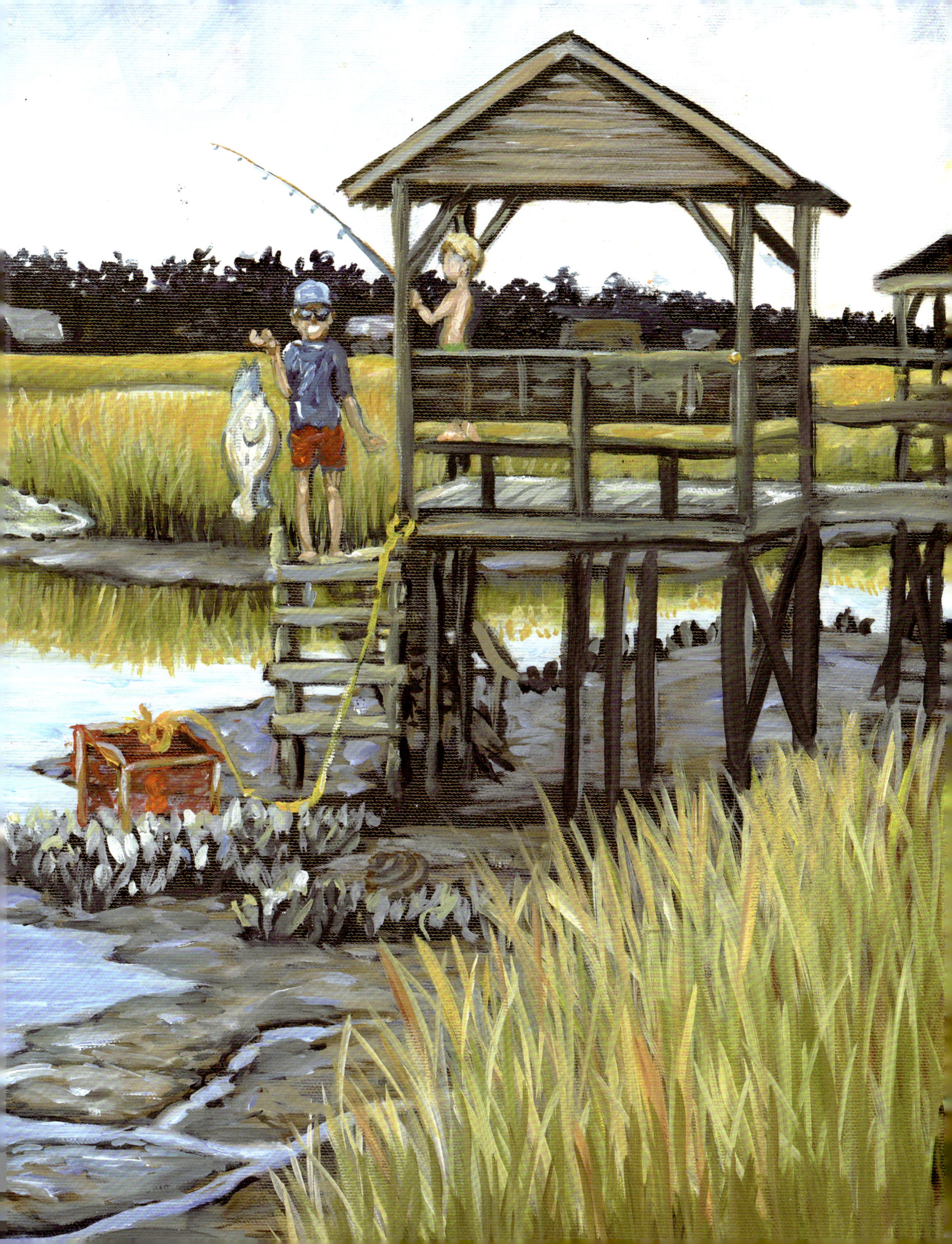

Goodnight **PAWLEYS** parade on the Fourth of July. Jets flying over and across the sky.

There's red, white, and blue and barbeque. Friends on the beach, some old some new. Sun goes down, no fireworks in town. We watch from a distance with no one around. This is such a special day. We all love our U. S A.

Goodnight **PAWLEYS** island it's the end of our stay. Wish we could spend just one more day. Packing up the car is not a bit fun. We would rather be playing in the sun. Goodbye **PAWLEYS** Island and friends from far and near. We can't wait to see you again next year.

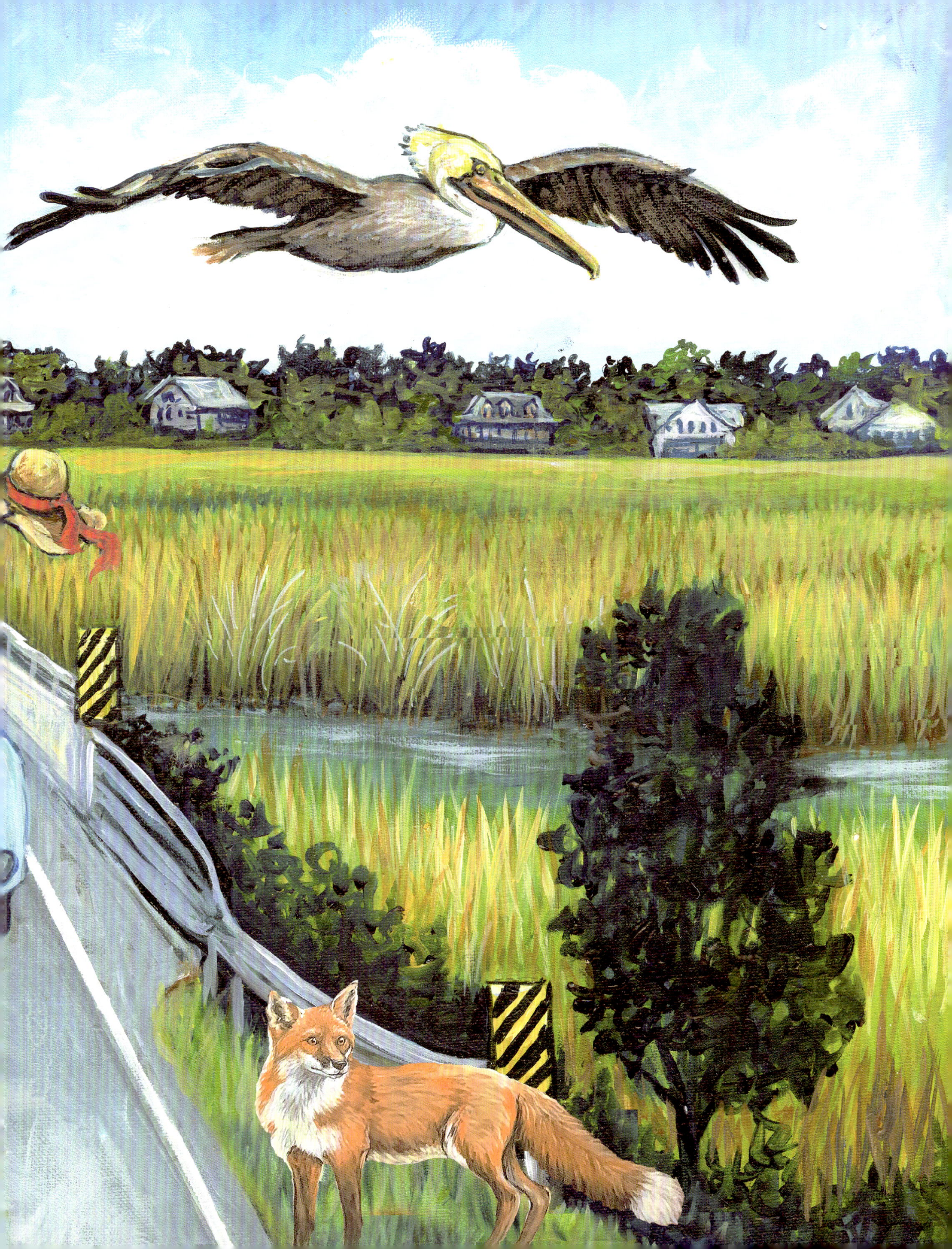

About the Artist...

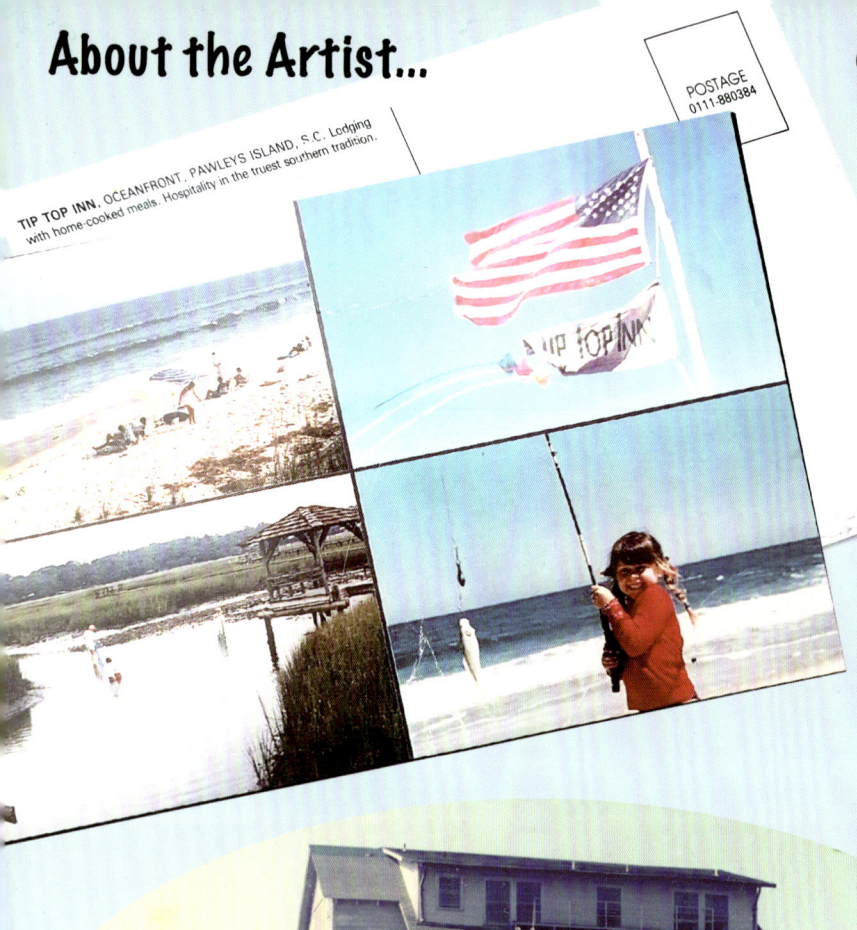

Keels Culberson Swinnie

Keels is a native of Pawleys Island and although her love of travel has taken her to many incredible places, she knows that there is nowhere like her beloved hometown. Her Godparents, Julian and Sis Kelly, owned the Tip Top Inn on Pawleys and her mother managed it, keeping Keels with her everyday as she worked. She had a magical childhood on Pawleys until Hurricane Hugo destroyed the Inn in 1989.

The love of art started at an early age for Keels. She underwent major hip surgery at the age of six and was in a full body cast. With the energy of a six year old and the inability to move, she channeled that energy into artistic endeavors and has been creating art ever since.

In 2004, Keels graduated from Converse College with a Bachelor of Fine Arts in Interior Design and Art History. She continued her education in Studio Art at the College of Charleston and the Santa Reparata International School of Art in Florence, Italy.

Keels now resides in downtown Georgetown, only 10 minutes away, with her husband and two little boys that love Pawleys almost as much as she does.

www.KeelsArt.com